COPING WITH UNAVOIDABLE STRESS:

Practices That Are Necessary for Building Emotional Resilience and Enhancing Overall Health

By

Charles Morales

Table of Content

6

Introduction

Everybody experiences stress, but we all manage it in different ways. One person's stress reaction trigger may not affect another. You can lessen the damaging effects of stress on your body and mind by learning good coping mechanisms.

I was motivated to create this book by my own experience with stress. Writing this book came about as a consequence of being admitted to the hospital and investigating the causes of my sickness. My quest for natural solutions to avoid the usual negative side effects of most psychotropic medicines, such as reduced brain function and danger to liver and kidney function, inspired and pushed me to continue in my work.

Using my academic research talents, I set out to learn all I could. I quickly understood that although I couldn't alter my inclination toward this severe and persistent mental disease, I could lower my chance of experiencing its symptoms. Developing emotional resilience, controlling the tension I couldn't completely eradicate, and lowering my level of stress were the three main components of that.

To be honest, at first, it was difficult. My everyday life consisted of balancing the responsibilities of being a single mother (with an out-of-state co-parent) with the demands of my full-time employment as a single mother of three children. All of this while attempting to fit in self-care activities like a simple beauty routine, an exercise program, a love of travel, and outdoor activities like hiking and kayaking.

I soon discovered that the frequency and intensity of my symptoms would probably force me into incapacity if I did not manage my stress. I therefore gained the ability to choose priorities and to live in the moment. Since then, I've discovered that the following factors are mostly responsible for my ability to keep up my health:

- *Regular exercise,*
- *Mindfulness practice,*
- *Nutritious diet,*
- *Enough sleep hygiene, and*
- *The companionship of people I love and who love me back.*

By taking these steps, I strengthened my emotional resilience and became more equipped to deal with emotional anguish and find a solution without endangering my physical or mental well-being.

I was requested to create a training on emotional resilience and given the chance to work as a mental health consultant for a Fortune 90 firm. My prepared materials served as the basis for stress management and compassion fatigue consulting practice. They served as the basis for this book as well as an inspiration for my first on stress management.

This book lists several typical stresses along with customized solutions. It centers on four primary techniques: Journaling, exercises focused on bodily motion, meditation, and mindfulness-based practices. You will be given specific activities that address the sorts of daily situations that might be causing tension in your life, along with instructions on how to recognize your stresses and triggers. To live a better and happier life at work and home, I hope you will use this book to create a set of customized methods that suit your particular pressures and reactions.

As you read the book, you may start to question if the tactics are helping. The majority of us are conscious of how we react to stress and can identify when we are experiencing stress. Our symptoms, which might range from intense perspiration to a sharp headache to dyspnea, are well known to us. We also know what quiet feels like sound sleep, clarity of mind, and attention. You won't become a Buddhist monk after putting the techniques in chapters two through six into practice, but you will experience relief from the most upsetting stress symptoms.

Chapter One

Fostering a Positive Connection with Stress

Stress affects us all, and it's not always a terrible thing. Stress in moderation might be beneficial! This chapter will cover the benefits of stress management and how to turn it into a force for good in our lives, as opposed to something that wears us out, depletes our energy, and leads to disease.

What Makes It Matter

Stress that we endure at times when we must perform at a high level, as during a crucial speech or game, is beneficial to us. It keeps our body prepared for a task and our minds alert and focused. However, our mind and body respond in an unhelpful manner when we are under constant stress or when we believe that a demanding circumstance is overwhelming us.

Stress often causes bodily symptoms that make us feel sick. It's important to understand that although we may not always control the things causing our stress, like a rigorous job schedule or a lengthy commute, we can manage how we react to it.

I can't guarantee that reading this book will make you a Zen master capable of handling life's stressors with composure and deep breathing. However, you will have the chance to pinpoint the particular stresses in your life and create effective stress-reduction plans. The following are some advantages of having a positive relationship with stress:

Inspires Mental Strength

The development of emotional resilience is essential to fostering a positive relationship with stress. This is the capacity to actively and imaginatively adjust to difficult circumstances and emergencies. Put differently, it's the way you recover from the challenging times. Developing emotional resilience helps your body and mind be ready for life's ups and downs so that, when they do occur, your responses won't have a detrimental effect on your life.

People are inherently resilient emotionally to some extent. Certain individuals are more susceptible to stress than others. Aside from our innate propensity to go for solace and tranquility when life becomes rough, there are additional traits that might influence our stress response. These consist of exposure to childhood trauma, gender, and age. The good news is that emotional resilience is something that can be achieved regardless of your genetic makeup.

The trio of emotional resilience encompasses:

- Physiological aspects, encompass physical wellness, vitality, and vigor.

- Cognitive or psychological components include self-management, self-worth, emotional consciousness, self-assurance, inner determination, adeptness in addressing challenges, adaptable mindset, attentiveness, and concentration.

- Interpersonal aspects comprise the quality of social bonds we maintain, like a nurturing circle of acquaintances, kin, and peers, and our degrees of affinity, collaboration, social integration, and interaction prowess.

Enhances Mental Development

The core tenet of a growth mindset is that by engaging in certain activities that strengthen our neural connections, the brain may develop.

Studies have shown that enhancing resilience by appropriate diet and sleep patterns might improve our neural networks and, therefore, the functioning of our brains.

Enhances Physical Well-Being

Physical health is also improved by healthily managing stress. According to research, one of the main reasons people see their primary care physician is stress. Cortisol release is one way that stress has a detrimental effect on health. While this is helpful in the short term, prolonged chronic inflammation may lead to blood vessel damage, aching joints, an increased risk of cardiovascular disease, and insulin resistance.

Asthma attacks, hypertension, and gastrointestinal conditions including heartburn, diarrhea, ulcers, acid reflux, constipation, and irritable bowel syndrome are some other physical reactions to stress. In addition, some individuals grind their teeth, have tension headaches, or have muscular pains. If left untreated, prolonged stress may have a significant negative impact on one's health. Because of this, developing stress management skills is a strong indicator of overall health and well-being. You are already well on your road to being happier and healthier if you are reading this book.

Brain Plasticity

The brain's central nervous system's capacity for lifelong learning and adaptation is known as neuroplasticity. "Neurons" is the abbreviation for "neuro." These nerve cells form the basis of our nervous system and the brain. The brain's capacity for adaptation is referred to as "plasticity." It is often referred to as neuro-elasticity or brain plasticity, and it describes the alterations in brain synapses and pathways brought about by interactions between neuronal processes.

It was thought, up until the 1960s, that the brain ceased growing during early childhood and infancy. Recent studies on the brain have shown that the brain may create new neural pathways and modify old ones in response to new experiences and information. Structural plasticity is the process by which the brain adapts to optimize function as we learn and develop throughout normal development.

This is best described as modifications to the brain's morphology brought about by learning. Age seems to influence this. Thus, throughout infancy and the early years of life, neurons and the synapses that link them expand quickly. But as we mature, we lose synapses because the ones we use often form stronger connections, while the ones we use are seldom likely to go.

This procedure is called synaptic pruning. Certain kinds of synapses in important brain regions are significantly reduced in several neurodegenerative disorders.

Neuroplasticity enables the brain to restore normal behavior in the event of an injury. For instance, language and motor function significantly improve in children who have had brain surgery to lessen seizures, and motor function may return after a stroke. These two instances illustrate the brain's capacity for "functional plasticity," or the transfer of a function from an injured to an uninjured location.

Guidelines For Use

You deal with stress in your life, just like almost everyone else on the earth. It might come from a lengthy commute, a demanding job that requires you to work long hours, parenting a troublesome adolescent, or caring for an aging parent. After all, it might be difficult to find time to take care of yourself and conduct errands when your dentist and dry cleaner are only available during the week.

Work may be difficult, even if you are one of the fortunate ones who can do it whenever and whenever you want. It is easy to lose track of when to work and when to relax when your workspace is a laptop and your meeting space is an online conference room. Additionally, the little time you have off from work can make you chronically exhausted and increase your risk of developing stress-related medical conditions if you live in the United States, today, except in a few states, there are no legally required maternity leave regulations or vacation time obligations.

These ailments could include anxiety, sadness, weight gain, migraine headaches, sleeplessness, hypertension, and gastrointestinal trouble.

Even if stress hasn't caused you to seek medical attention yet, you could notice an increase in your irritability and short fuse. What then can this book do for you? First of all, it's important to remember that stress may have a positive connection. It doesn't have to be your worst enemy, keep you up at night, and make you hate waking up in the morning. We will examine the relationship between the body and mind in this book, with particular attention to how stress affects your emotions, mind, and body. You'll discover fresh approaches to controlling and reducing the negative effects that stress has on your general well-being.

The most prevalent types of stress that individuals encounter will be covered, along with several scientifically proven methods for reducing stress that enhance mental health, prevent the detrimental effects of stress on the body, and foster emotional resilience. The answers in this book—movement, mindfulness, and psychology-based exercises—are what make it so important. These kinds of activities will assist you in developing a toolkit of techniques for mitigating the effects of stress in your life, enhancing mental and physical well-being, and fostering emotional resilience.

Scientifically Proven Physical Activities

One strategy for stress management, emotional resilience building, brain development, and physical health enhancement is thinking differently. Your way of thinking may lead to stress, such as worrying about whether your kid will succeed in 15 years or if you won't be able to sell to that group of people at your next meeting.

You may lessen your stress by changing the way you think. You're much more likely to experience less stress if you change your mindset from believing you will fail to believing you will achieve. "The greatest weapon against stress is our ability to choose one thought over the other," as American philosopher and pioneering psychology professor William James famously said.

Perhaps public speaking terrifies you. You're sure that nobody will listen to you or that you'll forget important details. Your palms start to perspire, your heart starts to beat, and you can't even concentrate on what you have to say because you spend so much time worrying about all the ways you will fail.

What if, instead, you concentrated on the fact that the crowd is really cheering you on and that you are an expert in your field and can enter the stage confidently rather than nervously?

By altering your thoughts, you may transform your life. You may utilize a variety of psychologically based coping mechanisms to handle the stresses in your life. Among them are:

Picturing the task. Performing a methodical mental walk-through, also known as visualization, of a task or occasion might be advantageous. Many elite athletes use visualization techniques to maximize their performance. American gymnast Simone Biles, for instance, has discussed working with a sports psychologist to hone her skills and get the confidence she needs to carry out very difficult athletic feats.

You are imagining serenity. Imagining a peaceful location or sensation may help you reduce stress symptoms by slowing your breathing, heart rate, and blood levels of cortisol and adrenaline. It may be anything you find soothing, such as the sensation you get after receiving a massage, lounging on your preferred beach, or taking in the quiet of a forest while on a stroll.

You are reciting affirmations or mantras. It has been shown that repeating words or mantras may improve emotional resilience by reshaping your self-perception. When you wake up every morning and see stickies on your bathroom mirror that showcase your strengths, for example, you begin to build emotional resilience by thinking positively about who you are and what you can do. Through this technique, you will force any doubts about your skills out of your head and replace them with thoughts of accomplishment.

Mindfulness-Based Practices

The issue of mindfulness is hard to escape these days as we become more aware of the stress that frequent distractions may cause. For instance, I had to log off of social media while writing this book. To avoid finding myself doing anything other than writing, which was what I needed to do, I carefully planned my email check-ins. To avoid receiving connection attempts, I enabled the Do Not Disturb function on my phone.

We can fully experience our lives when we practice mindfulness because it helps us stay focused on one thing at a time and completely in the present. It also enables us to work more efficiently and productively. Despite all of those advantages, many individuals still find it challenging to switch off their minds and pay attention to the present. Leading Buddhist meditation instructor and best-selling author Sharon Salzberg summarizes the practice by reminding us that "mindfulness isn't difficult, we just need to remember to do it."

Sometimes practicing mindfulness is as easy as closing your eyes and taking a long, deep breath. By doing so, you will increase blood oxygen levels, slow down breathing, and promote brain development by sharpening your attention and cognitive abilities. By putting you in more control of how you react emotionally to stressful situations—like a wailing child, nonstop emails, or heartbreaking news about a loved one—taking a deep breath also contributes to the development of emotional resilience.

Applying mindfulness to your eating may enhance digestion, lessen stress-related gastrointestinal symptoms like acid reflux, constipation, and indigestion, and increase your enjoyment of food by taking a lunch break and paying attention to the flavors and textures of your meal.

Exercises Focused on Bodily Motion

It was created for our bodies to move. But the current way of living is becoming more and more sedentary. Rather than going on a stroll, we use apps to purchase groceries and meals, or we take an Uber. We are in front of screens a lot—on TVs, computers, and phones, for example. The Centers for Disease Control and Prevention (CDC) reported in 2018 that between 2007 and 2016, the percentage of people who are obese climbed from 34 to 40 percent, while the percentage of people who are severely obese increased from 6 to 9 percent.

At least one in three persons, according to the World Health Organization, is overweight.

According to the organization, gaining weight is directly associated with a higher risk of heart disease, stroke, diabetes, some types of cancer, and musculoskeletal conditions like osteoarthritis.

One method to lower our risk of illness is to raise our physical activity levels. Even simple activities like walking may improve mental clarity and performance. Regular exercise, such as yoga, jogging, hiking, and other sports, strengthens emotional resilience by preparing your body and mind to withstand psychological or emotional suffering.

Acquiring proficiency in physical exercises may not only improve our physical health but also foster cognitive development. But even if you haven't made exercise a regular habit, you may utilize it as a better way to decompress when things become stressful. We'll cover a variety of stress-relieving techniques in this book, such as yoga, shoulder, and neck stretches, and fast walks around the block to get rid of extra energy. Enhancing mental well-being is a unique benefit of the sun and fresh air

Unpack The Complexities of Stress

Stress is your body's natural reaction to environmental changes. Physical, emotional, psychological, or behavioral changes are all possible. It is a condition of stress or strain in the mind or emotions brought on by difficult or demanding situations. It's the sensation that there's an excessive amount of psychological or emotional strain. You can do difficult activities and react to risk and danger effectively when you experience stress in tiny doses and at the appropriate moments. It could be a constructive way to deal with life's obstacles. Prolonged stress, nevertheless, is harmful to your health

Adrenaline and cortisol, the hormones produced during stressful events, may be harmful to the body and mind if they are continuously released for an extended length of time. It's also critical to understand that what stresses out one individual may not for another. Our socialization and hardwiring have conditioned us to react differently to stress.

First, let's discuss adrenaline (also known as epiphany). This hormone raises heart rate and respiration, which improves blood flow to the brain and muscles. It also starts the body's process of breaking down sugar so we may utilize it as fuel. All of this is done to enable us to react swiftly to whatever situation arises. The second major stress hormone that is produced following a stressful event is cortisol. The hormone lowers inflammation temporarily. On the other hand, long-term cortisol exposure may raise blood pressure, cholesterol, triglycerides, and sugar levels.

High amounts of cortisol may also cause plaque deposits to accumulate. All of this may result in insulin resistance, which may lead to diabetes, or damaged blood vessels, which may result in cardiovascular disease. Another possible outcome of ongoing stress is the development of painful joint conditions like arthritis. Prolonged stress exposure may both induce and aggravate diseases due to the effects of stress hormones on the body.

There are three main ways that stress affects our bodies:

Protect: Whether emotionally, mentally, or physically, we maintain our ground and protect ourselves.

Protect: Psychologically ignoring the cause of stress or physically leaving the room are two ways in which we could "run away."

Stop: Sometimes we get the sensation that we are physically anchored in one location as if our minds have "shut down" and we are unable to "think straight."

There are many different ways that stress affects our bodies. Minor symptoms may include heartburn, headaches, increased perspiration, rapid breathing, grinding teeth, diminished sex desire, or headaches. In addition to emotional and psychological reactions like anxiety, despair, irritation, and wrath, behavioral responses include things like smoking, drinking, and overeating or undereating.

Evolution of Stress Control

The Latin verb string, which means "to draw tight," is the root of the English term stress. Seems fitting considering the strain that stress causes in the body. The term "stress" is thought to have originated with the pioneering endocrinologist and stress theorist Hans Selye; in physics, it is defined as a force that exerts strain on a physical body. He claimed that stress had a deleterious effect on physical health and dubbed our body's reaction to stress as "general adaptation syndrome."

The goal of early stress research was to better understand homeostasis, or how our bodies maintain a steady environment. It looked into how our bodies were affected by the production of chemicals such as adrenaline and others when our minds perceived threats.

The effects of prolonged stress on the human psyche have been studied as a result of World War II military experiences. Selye's emphasis on physiological reactions was broadened by psychologist Richard Lazarus to include cognition and the emotions that follow, as well as the notion that coping functions as a stress response mediator. Scientific developments have made it possible to quantify the amount of stress hormones in various settings.

According to the study, everyone's stress hormones were raised in response to three typical situations: novelty, unpredictability, and danger to one's ego and sense of control, or NUTS. Researchers started examining the body's and mind's reactions to stress around the 1980s. The definition of post-traumatic stress disorder was broadened to include experiences of isolated or ongoing violence in a variety of contexts, including the community or household. During this period, pharmacological and behavioral therapies were developed as a result of new insights into the physiological and molecular elements of stress.

In the twenty-first century, stress is intensively researched in both the scientific and social sciences, ranging from chemistry and biology to psychology and anthropology, and it is now acknowledged as a normal aspect of everyday living. This covers research on prenatal stress, how it affects a fetus's development, how it foretells health issues in later life, and how it affects future generations.

Main Categories of Stress

Acute and chronic stress are the two main categories of stress that are often discussed. You may encounter both kinds throughout your lifetime.

Understanding the distinctions between the two and the approaches for handling each is crucial.

Being able to identify the different kinds of stress you are experiencing will help you handle it better and do the least amount of damage to your body and mind.

In keeping with that, it's also important to talk about the biochemistry of stress and how your body reacts to and adjusts to it. Understanding how stress affects your body can help you reduce any harmful effects that may arise in the long run. Let's examine the many forms of stress and how our bodies react to stress in our surroundings.

Acute Stress

It probably wouldn't take you long to jot down a list of the things in your life that give you stress. Let's talk about the work commute. Some individuals may find a quiet place to unwind while on public transportation, either by listening to music or audiobooks or by napping. Some find the loudness and the throng to be unsettling. While some individuals joyfully listen to their favorite podcast or morning talk program or even sing along to their favorite music, others may find themselves in fits of road rage, shouting at other cars. Major life events like getting married or divorced, starting a new career or being unemployed, having a kid, or losing a loved one may also result in acute stress.

This kind of tension passes quickly. Acute stress symptoms disappear when the stressor is removed, over time, or via self-management. Severe stress causes your heart rate to increase, perspiration to appear on your hands, and breathing to quicken. You can get knots in your stomach or struggle to fall or remain asleep. Being overstimulated with cortisol and adrenaline is the cause of this. In addition, you can feel more conscious and awake as a result, which will prepare you for the task at hand.

After the stressful incident has passed, your body will achieve homeostasis and the hormones that cause stress will return to normal.

Chronic Stress

Chronic stress, in contrast to acute stress, is constant. An excellent illustration would be if you wake up in the morning anxious about your impending commute. You arrive at work to find a packed schedule that makes it seem impossible to get anything done on your to-do list. Chronic stress may also arise from long-term financial difficulties or from caring for a parent or kid who is unwell.

Your body is continuously overloaded with hormones and equilibrium never returns after prolonged stress. It's this kind of tension that leads to weight gain and persistent sleeplessness. In addition to causing persistent muscular tension, chronic stress is linked to the development of type 2 diabetes and cardiovascular disease.

Typical Stressors

Although stress is quite individual, most of us have at some point encountered certain pressures.

Finances/Money. In many parts of the nation, living expenses are rising much more quickly than incomes. Budgets might also be strained by significant family debt and school debts. Finally, the growth of the "gig economy" brings with it irregular and erratic earnings.

Work: The American Psychological Association states that the primary cause of stress is one's place of employment. Extended work hours, few vacations, and a "always on" work ethic made possible by technology are common characteristics of modern work cultures.

Family and home. It's possible that your family isn't receiving as much attention as you would want to if you are always at work. Frequently, you could feel fatigued or preoccupied even if you do have time for them. What stage your family is in right now will also determine how stressed out you are about family matters. Because of their lack of sleep and continual emotional and physical demands, infants may be quite tired. Other forms of chronic stress may be brought on by tweens and adolescents who are experimenting with becoming independent.

Health/Wellness: Because of the complicated medical systems and expensive therapy associated with them, chronic health issues may also be quite stressful, particularly in the United States.

Principal Players like Stress

There is no distinction between the body and the mind when it comes to stress. Rarely, you won't have behavioral and emotional symptoms in addition to physical ones, or the other way around. We no longer often confront predators in the contemporary world. However, our bodies continue to react to events that our brain interprets as potentially fatal, like an oncoming automobile as we're trying to cross the street. Now factor in a 12-hour workday after an extremely short sleep schedule. The body will probably overreact and produce a tonne of chemicals as a consequence, including cortisol and adrenaline (epinephrine).

Thus, how does this incredible chemical process take place? Our bodies alert the amygdala, an almond-shaped collection of neurons in the temporal lobe of the brain when they sense a danger via our eyes, hearing, or other organs. It is a component of the limbic system, which is in charge of learning, motivation, arousal, emotions, and memories. The brain's limbic system consists of many regions, including the thalamus, hippocampus, hypothalamus, and amygdala.

Stress Response Center

The amygdala is critical to your ability to feel a range of emotions. Additionally, it enhances your ability to identify emotions in other people and prepares you for a reaction, or the fight-or-flight response, before other brain regions can determine whether you should be afraid or not. The hypothalamus releases corticotropin-releasing hormone (CPH), a pituitary-adrenal stress hormone, in response to stimulation of the amygdala by a stressful experience.

Two other crucial stress hormones, cortisol, and adrenaline, are released by the adrenal gland in response to this hormone. The control of our emotional, psychological, and physical reactions to stimuli depends on the release of stress hormones. Excessive amounts of stress hormones might cause temporary harm to brain connections. Exercise is one of the many activities that might enable your brain to heal and form new connections because of its plasticity.

Epinephrine

The body is prepared for an emergency when adrenaline is released because it improves respiration and blood pressure while rerouting blood flow from the skin and digestive system to the muscles and brain. Many refer to this as an "adrenaline rush." Your heart rate will rise as a result. When breathing, the hormone widens the lungs' tiny airways, allowing more oxygen to enter. This increase in oxygen to the brain sharpens senses, making pupils in the eyes larger and heightening attentiveness

An excessive amount of adrenaline may be harmful to your heart and other organs and cause symptoms including sweating, fast breathing, and palpitations in the heart.

The Steroid Co

Cortisol is a normal aspect of the body's reaction to stimuli in moderation. After a stressful incident, it aids in the body's return to equilibrium by controlling blood pressure, the immune system, and the metabolism of proteins, carbs, and fat, as well as having an anti-inflammatory effect. The body produces more cortisol than it can use while under continuous or chronic stress.

When it reaches high concentrations, it might hinder vital biological processes, such as the development of insulin resistance in cells. Type 2 diabetes is the result of elevated blood sugar levels and weight gain brought on by this. Additionally, it may cause the amygdala to enlarge and the prefrontal cortex to atrophy. The body becomes more vulnerable to stress as a result of this response, which feeds a vicious cycle that keeps the brain in a nearly continual state of light or dark.

The Central Nervous System

Through the pituitary gland, which hangs from the hypothalamus by a thin "thread," the hypothalamus communicates with the neurological and endocrine systems. The hypothalamus, which is found near the base of the brain, is also known as the master switchboard because it regulates the endocrine system and is essential for the body to remain balanced. It does this by managing the endocrine and neurological reactions to stimuli. It does this by stimulating or inhibiting vital bodily processes including body temperature, respiration, cardiac regulation, appetite, thirst, sleep, and circadian rhythms

This controls the autonomic nerve system, which is responsible for controlling the heartbeat, breathing, and other involuntary behaviors. It also controls blood pressure, vasomotor activity, and some elements of parenting and bonding behaviors.

Major Brain Regions

The cerebrum, cerebellum, and brain stem are the three distinct components that make up the brain. The brain's processing of stress and the body's hormone release occur in the cerebrum.

Stress Builds Up in the Body

Known as our "weight or light" reflex, the brain releases hormones throughout the body in response to stress as a defensive strategy. Chronic stress may be harmful to the body over time, impairing many organs and systems.

Cognitive Control Region

The prefrontal cortex is another area of the brain implicated in the stress response. It is the most developed area of the brain and is in charge of sophisticated cognitive functions. This is when rational decision-making begins. It's interesting to note that this area of the brain doesn't completely mature until people are in their mid-twenties, which helps to explain why teens often act recklessly and make bad decisions.

The Indices and Signs of Infertility Reduction of Stress

As you now know, both short-term and long-term stress triggers a range of brain responses to inputs that underlie physical, emotional, and psychological reactions. But, by using the appropriate tactics, you may step in and either stop or slow down the chain reaction that deteriorates our health. Let's talk about some of the reactions to stress and how they show up in our day-to-day activities first.

Burnout and Stress

After the body has reacted to severe stress, it takes the hormones around 30 minutes to fade away, causing the physical and mental responses to stop. Chronic stress, on the other hand, keeps the body primed and makes you feel worn out. Fatigue might result from the elevated blood pressure, fast breathing, and heightened physical and mental awareness these factors produce.

It's like waiting for the gun to go off at the starting line of a race, except it never does. Your muscles are taut, waiting for that moment to release their tension, but eventually, you get exhausted from this heightened physical response. Tension also persists since stress does not go away. It may manifest as headaches, strained neck, and shoulder muscles, or grinding of the teeth.

Insomnia

It is difficult to relax and fall asleep while you are in a state of heightened awareness brought on by adrenaline, regardless of the cause of your stress. It might be difficult to fall or keep asleep, for instance, if a disagreement with a friend or family member isn't settled before going to bed. Sleep deprivation has both short- and long-term effects on your body and mind, making you less equipped to handle stress.

Despair and Worry

When circumstances seem overwhelming, melancholy and anxiety may result from chronic stress. For instance, you can experience anxiety or depression if you are having financial difficulties and don't know how to raise your income. Simple actions like heading to the mailbox, where you know late notifications are waiting for you, might exacerbate these emotions even more. Moreover, the inability to get enough sleep may lead to despair and anxiety, and the opposite is also true. Developing regular sleep hygiene, or sleep-training behaviors, is crucial to developing emotional resilience.

Body Weight Adjustment

Insulin resistance might result from excessive cortisol levels. Weight gain is the consequence of the body storing extra fat in your cells due to an excess of insulin. Depending on what your body requires, the hypothalamus may either stimulate or suppress thirst or hunger. It also controls the body's homeostasis system. Stress eating, commonly referred to as increased appetite, is a common reaction in many individuals to stress.

Foods that are heavy in fat, salt, or sugar, such as ice cream or potato chips, usually provide comfort to people. It is simple to understand how stress might result in weight gain when you combine stress eating with insulin resistance and a sluggish metabolism. On the other hand, some individuals lose weight while under stress because they have less of an appetite.

Severe and Prolonged Illness

It makes sense that those who suffer from severe and chronic diseases should experience stress. However, persistent and severe diseases may also be brought on by stress. As was previously mentioned, overdosing on cortisol and adrenaline may cause a variety of health problems. Inflammation and lowered immunity may result in lifelong and dangerous conditions such as diabetes (due to insulin resistance brought on by excessive cortisol), hypertension (because of elevated adrenaline levels), and heart disease.

Before Starting

This book will provide you with the skills to control your physical, emotional, and psychological reactions, which will help you deal with the stressful events in your life. Some of these tactics will be your deliberate reactions to stressful events that happen to you in the present. Others who are physically and emotionally fit to handle everyday obstacles and more acute unforeseen encounters can assist you in developing your resistance to stress. For instance, taking a long, deep breath might settle your heart and help you feel composed enough to create a strong impact if you are ready to conduct a crucial meeting and you can feel your palms starting to perspire.

The key to implementing a long-term stress management plan daily is cultivating a mindfulness practice. This might include walking or any other regular workout regimen. Maintaining your physical and emotional well-being while keeping your body prepared for any situation is the aim. These strategies may assist you in getting through a difficult period in your life, such as a divorce, unemployment, or the loss of a loved one.

Having a diary is a good idea if you want to complete the writing prompts in this book since many of the exercises it suggests will require you to have writing supplies available. As you prepare for chapters two through six, you may wish to purchase a unique pen just for this procedure to make it more special.

Unavoidable Stress

Chapter Two

Managing Daily Difficulties

For the majority of us, the never-ending responsibilities of everyday living are what causes us stress rather than major life events. Indeed, our brains are programmed to respond to actual threats like lions or fires, but they also seem to operate similarly when we are caught in traffic on our everyday commute to and from work.

Frantic Conversation

You're probably all too acquainted with the stressful journey to and from work that occurs in the morning and evening. You know the anxiety of leaving early just to be stuck in a parking lot while traveling on the interstate. Despite your best efforts to remain composed, you can't help but glance at the clock and wish that you wouldn't be late.

Mindfulness-Based Practices

Now that you've been using your blinker to indicate a lane change for some time, what can you do the next time someone cuts you off or accelerates to the point where you are unable to merge? You may want to try practicing mindfulness. First, let's talk about your breath. Stress affects the respiratory system, and shallow, fast breathing is often a first indication that you've gone too far emotionally or mentally. The idea is to pay attention to your body as you breathe.

1. *As you sit up straight in your chair, take a steady, five-count breath in through your nose.*
2. *Blow out through your lips on a count of five.*
3. *Pay attention to the sensation of your breath entering your lungs via your nose when you inhale; pay attention to how your diaphragm*

expands as your body fills with air and contracts when your breath leaves your body.

4. Repeat this five times until your body begins to relax.

Concentrating on a mantra is the second helpful mindfulness practice that lets you pay attention to your driving. You may enter a meditative state with the use of a mantra, which is a phrase or sound that you repeat. It works by substituting a more soothing word for obsessive, unpleasant thoughts.

To "check out" of the outside world and concentrate within, you would normally shut your eyes. However, please do not do this when operating a motor vehicle. Rather, this mantra will assist you in being relaxed and composed, ensuring that thoughts of driving anger are banished.

1. As a mantra, any word or phrase will do. "I get there when I get there," maybe.
2. For as long as necessary, and for at least five minutes, repeat the sentence.

Time Boundaries/ Deadlines

Not every busy CEO with a lengthy list of deliverables and a staff to assist, mentor, and motivate is immune to the perils of deadlines. Deadlines also affect students who must balance the conflicting demands of midterms and final exams, as well as stay-at-home parents who must arrange their children's schedules and finances. Regardless of your circumstances, having an excessive number of deadlines might leave you feeling as if you won't be able to do everything unless you can multitask.

Practice Journaling

Putting problems on paper via writing is a terrific method to let go of them. Writing may inspire greatness in you since the first step to realizing your ideas and aspirations is to put them into words. This writing exercise shows you how to prioritize your goals, honor your accomplishments, and establish a connection with your emotions. You will need a calendar for this activity so that you can plan out your obligations. Additionally, a notebook to record your emotions will be needed.

1. Make a list of everything you need to get done in the next month, including deadlines, and write it down on the first page of your diary.
2. After entering everything into the calendar, stop and consider your sentiments for a moment. At the bottom of the list, put three words that best capture your feelings.

3. Write down the tasks you need to do in the next week along with the days and times they are due underneath the list.

4. Examine the list; what can be postponed for a few days and what may be eliminated since it's not that important?

5. Draw a line across the objects that don't need your immediate attention. Poof! You now have a reduced list.

6. Now that your list is smaller, take a minute to jot down three words that best express how you are feeling.

7. If any chores can wait, note them down and schedule a time or day in the next weeks to get started. Alternatively, go ahead and prioritize your list of the top five projects for the week.

8. Place a checkmark next to each assignment or activity as you finish it. When finished, write a

word of celebration next to each item and make a note of the date and time.

Sleeping Difficulties for Your Child

The grueling nature of caring for a child is well-known to those who have experienced it. Toddlers are establishing their identities, learning to be independent, and fervently wanting to have their way. And before bed is one of their favorite moments to show off their independence. Even adults often go to bed to watch TV, check social media, or respond to emails that can wait until the next morning, so you can easily appreciate your two-year-old's perspective

Practice Meditation

Changing the way you think about your child might help relieve some of the tension associated with sleep. How do they proceed?

Engaging in play? Being obliging? Any toddler's developmental stage includes this. You might start to see this power struggle quite differently if you realize that it's a necessary aspect of their development. While going to bed won't become any simpler by magic, it won't be as emotionally draining as it could otherwise b

1. First, acknowledge your affection for your toddler—the incredible human being you can't wait to see grow and change

2. When you're having moments of resistance that are driving you crazy, keep reminding yourself of that love.

3. Telling your child how much you love them throughout the nighttime ritual can help you stay focused on that love.

4. Change your perspective to see how you are assisting your kid in maturing and growing throughout this specific challenge.

   By doing this, you may help kids learn self-control and regularity in their lives.

5. You'll discover that keeping your attention on the love you have for that little person transforms nighttime from a time for yet another battle to an occasion to reflect, experience, and express your love for your kid

Housework Conflicts

Even though I am in my 60s, I can still clearly recall how much I disliked doing my homework as a youngster. I wanted to watch TV instead. In addition, even though my daughter is in her 20s, I can still clearly recall what it meant to make sure her schoolwork was completed on time. Any conflict with a youngster demands a composed, concentrated, and in-control mentality. It is useless to shout at your kid, get irate, or use punishment to make them do something they don't want to.

You will both be exhausted and angry by the time it is finished.

Mindfulness-Based Practices

To assist you both in concentrating and de-stressing so that you can work together to solve the intellectual obstacle that lies ahead, do this mindfulness practice. Additionally, it will establish a homework schedule that begins with harmony rather than hostility.

1. Choose a few songs to include in your assignment playlist together. Save the tracks to your preferred music player. Alternatively, you may choose a certain kind of music that you stream as your "homework channel."

2. Select a calming and soothing kind of music, such as jazz, new age, or classical.

3. Set a timer on your phone and spend at least five minutes listening to the music together before your youngster begins working on the project.

4. Shut your eyes and clasp your hands.

5. Determine which instruments are being performed or concentrate on what the spoken words signify.

6. Once you and your kid have listened for five minutes, continue the music while you do your assigned "homework" and your youngster completes their homework.

Dining Time

Getting supper on the table for a lot of working folks often entails having something delivered or picking it up on the way home. Although it's more expensive, it's also a lot less stressful than trying to figure out what's in the fridge on your way home from work so you can prepare a hot supper for your family. But making supper on a weekday doesn't have to be a stressful or rushed process.

Practice Journaling

Creating meal choices that make you look forward to dinnertime rather than dread it is the main goal of this activity. Meal planning is a tedious but necessary daily activity that you may feel more in control of by devoting a little time to it.

1. Note down the items you have in your pantry and refrigerator in a notepad or diary.

2. Consider what you would want to prepare for supper.

3. List three products that you may use as the centerpiece of your dinner that are currently in your refrigerator. Although a protein may be the

most convenient to highlight, anything might serve as the meal's centerpiece.

4. Decide on only one dish to prepare for supper that day.

5. Give a brief explanation of the method you wish to use to prepare that main meal, such as baking, frying, or steaming it.

6. List the seasonings you want to use for your main meal and outline the actions you will take to get it ready for cooking.

7. List the two side dishes you would want to serve with your dinner, along with the steps involved in their preparation

Once you've finished these steps, you're ready to prepare supper, but this time you have a plan instead of feeling overwhelmed.

Domestic Task

As the laundry or bathroom won't clean or wash itself, doing the chores is one of those adulting activities that we must all do. Given that, you may as well enjoy yourself while completing tasks by taking advantage of this mobility chance.

Exercises Focused on Bodily Motion

Instead of making you feel anxious about cleaning, this activity will get you moving and into a positive frame of mind. When you do all of your duties, your home will be neater and cleaner, and you will have accomplished the tasks while enjoying your favorite music, which will put you in a cheerful mood. In addition, your daily step count will have increased by a significant amount. Thank you very much.

1. Start by turning on your favorite dancing music—whatever it is that makes you happy and smile and makes you want to move your feet and hips.

2. Take out the vacuum, broom, mop, or duster and team up with it as you dance through the task at hand.

3. Picture yourself dancing with your favorite star.

4. When you've finished.

5. Perform a joyous dance while cleaning, sweeping, or vacuuming if it makes you feel like you're ready for Dancing with the Stars.

6. When the next song begins, spin around the room to hear it through. After that, it will be time to begin duty number two.

7. When it's time to clean the restroom, sing along and scrub the bathtub or toilet to the beat of the song.

8. Continue in the kitchen, and so forth, but make sure you dance in between each task.

Children's Welfare

The days of kids sitting out at home watching their favorite program or playing in parks, playgrounds, and backyards after school are long gone. Many kids these days have a calendar full of events that demand them to be somewhere other than their parents. Naturally, cutting back on the activities kids participate in is one strategy to lessen this stressor. But, if there are multiple children involved, the where, when, and how logistics can become even more challenging, regardless of the quantity of activities they offer.

Mindfulness-Based Practices

When the mere thought of your child's weekend and after-school activities overwhelms you, it's time to practice mindfulness.

The goal of this practice is to center and calm you, making it impossible for stress, misplaced belongings, or even a child's tantrum to affect you.

1. It makes no difference if you are standing, sitting, or lying down—just start by remaining motionless.

2. Take a five-minute break (make sure your phone is in Do Not Disturb mode before setting the timer).

3. Shut your eyes and inhale deeply through your nose, then release the breath through your mouth. Imagine a stunning location in a natural environment that you have visited and enjoyed

or a place you have never been but have always wanted to go.

4. Imagine yourself strolling and savoring the beauty of the surroundings while you are there. Take in the sights, sounds, and aromas while maintaining a feeling of tranquility.

5. Imagine yourself in the imagined scene, finding a spot to sit and concentrating on just one object. Keep doing this until the timer sounds.

Open your eyes when the alarm goes off. The brief mental vacation you had will make you feel refreshed and at ease.

Challenges with Workplace Workers

If you have never had to collaborate with someone challenging, count yourself fortunate. Whether you wake up smiling and eager for the day ahead or with a feeling of dread and concern about what lies ahead, it may all be attributed to a demanding colleague.

Practice Journaling

This is an activity designed to help you concentrate on the good aspects of your work. Despite that difficult colleague, it serves as a reminder of all the great things about your job and the lovely individuals you work with. You won't be concentrating on that challenging colleague once you do this workout. Knowing that they are just a little drawback to a huge positive will give you the confidence to cope with them.

1. Begin by heading a new page in your diary, "Why I Love My Job."
2. Jot down the below expressions and complete the missing word in each one:

This is why I applied for the job: ....

I was relieved to be hired because my goal was to

……… …… …… …… …,,,,,,,,,,,,,,,,,,,,,,,,,,,

"This is why I enjoy going to work every day:

……… …… …… …… …,,,,,,,,,,,,,,,,,,,,,,,,,,,

"I like ……………………,,,,,,,,,,,,,,,,,,,,,,,,,,,the most at work because ………………,,,,,,,,,,,,,,,,,,,,,,,,,,,."

"I'm eager to start work today because I'm looking forward to ………………,,,,,,,,,,,,,,,,,,,,,,,,,,,."

3. After finishing the final sentence, review your writing from the beginning.

4. Carry out step four again.

5. Now, complete it by going to work (or returning to work, depending on when you are doing this).

Chapter Three

Overcoming Innovative Situations

Living involves experiencing new things. Every day is unique from the moment we are born. It is reasonable to suggest that as you get older, you'll go through several exhilarating and frightening—and sometimes both at once—life-altering changes. We seldom avoid these situations, thus it's more crucial to concentrate on how you handle your emotions throughout them.

New Job Opportunity

Your life's most thrilling event could have been when you finally landed the job for which you had spent so much time applying and interviewing. Joyousness! But as the party ends, fear about making new friends and learning new tasks at work creeps in along with reality. Even if you're still thrilled, you can get a bit anxious. Until you get the swing of things, you can experience anxiety.

Mindfulness-Based Practices

Including regular meditation practice in your morning routine is one of the finest strategies to get psychological and emotional serenity. Being calm, focused, and mentally clear when you wake up is a powerful emotional and mental boost. It not only increases productivity but also strengthens your ability to handle stress from unforeseen chores that may arise during the day. As a pick-me-up to help you through the remainder of the day, you may even repeat it at lunch.

Additionally, affirmations—statements you make aloud or, depending on your situation, internally—that express an emotion you want to achieve—will be a part of this activity. It might be more specific, like "I will close at least one deal today," or it can be as generic as "I will be awesome at work today."

1. Start by deciding on the phrase you want to use for your affirmation.

2. Assume the lotus stance by sitting on the floor (or in your chair, depending on where you are working) with your legs crossed and your hands resting on your thighs with your palms facing up.

3. Shut your eyes and inhale deeply through your lips and out of your nose.

4. Continue inhaling deeply as you make ten repetitions of your affirmation.

5. Breathe deeply through your nose and out through your lips for the last affirmation.

6. Shut your eyes and get going for the day.

I can assure you that starting a regular meditation practice will change how you see the difficulties you face each day.

Purchasing a New House

Best wishes on your new residence! You're undoubtedly eager to use your interior design talents to set up each area just as you want. In addition to having to learn how to adapt to a new environment, I imagine you're also stressed about connecting utilities and getting to know your new neighbors.

Practice Journaling

Writing is best done during transitions. You may communicate your feelings, your hopes, and the things you're glad you left behind by doing this. As you put your aspirations on paper, this writing activity will construct a kind of text-based vision board.

Write a diary entry explaining your decision to make this location your new home.

- *Which part of the listing caught your eye?*
- *What caught your attention throughout the tour?*

Do you have any aspirations for this house?

- *What types of pursuits are you hoping to engage in at your new residence?*
- *Which memories are you hoping to make? Who do you think will visit?*
- *Are there any future adjustments you would want to make?*
- *Do you want to remodel your kitchen, bathroom, or bedroom?*

- *Do you envision your ideal shed?*

- *Would you want the landscape to be rearranged? Do you want to grow more?*

You will feel more connected to your house and will concentrate on what makes it home after completing this writing activity. You may use what you write as a road map for your house's future.

Leaving the Workforce

The day has finally come when you don't have to get up early on Mondays to go to work. Praise be! You can also be anxious about the significant transition that comes with giving up the activities that have governed your life's rhythm for the last four to five decades. How then should one use all that time? A fitness regimen is a great way to begin the rest of your life.

Exercises Focused on Bodily Motion

Let's move your body and make the most of your additional time. Stretching your whole body is a great way to begin and finish the day. Stretching may help you unwind in the evening before going to bed and keep you feeling limber and prepared for the day's activities. In addition to helping you stay strong and flexible as you age, stretching may also help you avoid breaks and falls. (Please remember that you should speak with your healthcare professional before starting any new stretching program if you have any physical limits or injuries.)

1. Assume a standing position with your feet shoulder-width apart.
2. Extend your arms over your head to the furthest extent possible, bringing your palms together.
3. Inhale deeply through your nose and exhale through your mouth three times.

4. After that, bend at the waist and stretch as far to the right as you can while lowering your right arm to your side. Breathe deeply three times.

5. Repeat by taking three deep breaths, extending your left arm to your side, putting your right arm as near to your head, and stretching as far as you can to your left.

6. Take three deep breaths and come back to the center with your arms over your head.

7. Unwind. Your body should feel loose and flexible, and you should feel grounded and at ease.

Entrance Into School

A fresh academic career might elicit a range of feelings. The thought of all you will discover and the people you will meet excites me. Moreover, it may cause worry for the same reasons. No matter how you feel, going to college may be difficult.

Maintaining composure, motivation, and attention is crucial to finishing all of your projects on time without losing your mind.

Mindfulness-Based Practices

Engaging in mindfulness exercises is a great way to feel in control and prepared to face the challenges of college life. When the rigors of school are making you feel nervous or overburdened, you may go back to this exercise. This practice will help you become more focused and will also serve as a mental check-in for when you need to take a break. This counting practice may be done anywhere and at any time.

1. Look for a peaceful area with little outside disturbances.
2. Assume a shoulder-width apart stance.

3. Shut your eyes and inhale deeply and slowly through your nose, then exhale slowly through your mouth. Count by fives gradually until you get to 100. (Try counting in groups of threes to help you concentrate.)

4. After you've finished your slow count to 100, open your eyes and resume your necessary tasks, making the most of your increased attention.

You have to put your issues aside for this exercise and concentrate just on counting. It's also a fantastic method to get your mind ready for difficult work.

Marriage

Cheers to a long life filled with love, happiness, and delight spent together. You are embarking on an exciting new chapter in your life. Regardless of whether you've previously been married or cohabiting, this new status might affect how you communicate with your spouse.

Practice Journaling

A fresh start in life is an excellent moment to jot down your aspirations and goals for the future. This might include trying out new hobbies or simply adopting a different outlook on life. The goal of this practice is to help you move forward from fear about what lies ahead to loving and good sentiments.

1. Together with your spouse, make a list of your shared life goals.

- *About what are you ecstatic?*

- *What fears do you have?*

- *What standards do you hold yourself and your spouse to in terms of behavior? For instance, what tasks will be performed by whom?*

2. After that, make a list of how you see your life together in a year.

- *Are you going to stay at the same address?*

- *Do you want a pet or do you want to have children?*

3. What are your long-range objectives? After five years, how does your married life seem to be?

- *Have you visited any of the places on your bucket list?*

- *Is it time for a new automobile or another child?*

4. Imagine your life ten years from now with your new partner.

- *Have you established any new customs or rituals within the family that align with your principles?*

- *Which nations are you going to visit together?*

Relocating To Another Place

You just started a new job and are relocating to a new city, where you may or might not know anybody. Regardless of the cause of your relocation, relocating is an arduous undertaking. There are the laborious chores of packing, unpacking, and other moving-related activities.

Practice Meditation

It seems sense that you would want to do nothing more than get into bed, pull the covers over your head, and pray that everything gets done without you. Regretfully, however, you will still need to oversee the procedure even if you have given specialists the task of packing and heavy lifting. Getting oneself in the proper frame of mind, or ending and beginning the day in a tranquil condition, is the problem here. Keep in mind that thoughts influence feelings.

- Convert your viewpoint from one of pessimism to optimism; emphasize all the positive possibilities rather than just the negative ones. There's no sense fretting about things that go wrong because they will.

- Consider this relocation as a new experience that will provide personal and professional progress, rather than as a new place to meet people.

- Problem-solving will be simpler if you are in a positive frame of mind than if you engage in catastrophe thinking. This will greatly facilitate and improve the transition throughout your relocation.

Changing Occupational Paths

You have plenty to be proud of if you've effectively promoted yourself in a new field and are starting a new profession. Go to you, this is not simple work! While some level of worry is understandable at this point in your life, let's make sure that fear doesn't follow you around all the time.

Practice Meditation

It may seem impossible to find time for anything else due to the mental strain of learning a new function in a new field. Making time for mindfulness, however, can improve your productivity, attention, mental clarity, and creativity—all fantastic traits to help you kill it in your new work. There is an activity you can take at work that can boost your productivity and efficiency.

At least twenty minutes should pass throughout this mindfulness exercise. That implies no emails or phone calls. If you would rather practice under guidance, you may access mindfulness or meditation websites on your computer or phone. Put a 20-minute timer on your phone.

1. Create a motto to help you stay focused on achieving success in your new profession.

2. Put your phone away and set it to the Do Not Disturb mode. Alternatively, turn it face down on your desk or table and ask your assistant to take messages for the next 20 minutes if they handle your calls. If you aren't able to get a private workstation, think about using a conference or break room.

3. If listening to music or wearing earbuds helps in concentration, do this without the guidance of a prompt.

4. Now go to work and begin saying your mantra aloud. If your thoughts stray, don't forget to return them to your chant.

5. After 20 minutes, walk around for five minutes to get your blood flowing and give your brain a chance to rest.

6. Make use of this opportunity to use the restroom or rehydrate with some fluids. Going outdoors for a little while and breathing in some fresh air will also help your mental state.

Disengagement

Breaking up is hard to do," as stated in the song, is accurate. To put it simply, this is true whether you are the one being dumped or the one performing the dumping. Using writing as therapy is an excellent practice to help you get through this difficult period.

Practice Journaling

Take part in a writing activity that puts your relationship in perspective to declutter your thoughts and heal your heart. You can be receptive and ready to give love another try in the future by putting your ideas in writing. Most likely, you are mired in your emotions and mentally reliving certain instances while obsessing over the areas in your relationship where you went wrong. Through a methodical examination of your relationship, this activity will help you go from your heart to your brain by perhaps bringing closure and making sense of what transpired.

1. Consider all the positive aspects of your relationship and jot down, on paper, at least one page listing them. (At least one page, yes.) Pay attention to the relationship's dynamics. Jot down all that you both done to contribute to the happy, gratifying, and rewarding nature of your relationship. Though it could seem challenging and perhaps counterproductive, the goal of this

exercise is to help you understand why you choose to spend time with this individual. It also lessens possibilities for self-criticism when you make decisions you believe were incorrect and lets you concentrate on the positive aspects of the relationship rather than getting bogged down in everything that went wrong.

2. Next, consider the issues that arose in the relationship and write in your notepad or diary for no more than two pages. It's crucial to keep your page count down here since it's so simple to be drawn into the negativity. Try to keep your attention on what went wrong with you rather than what the other person did wrong. Pay attention to the dynamics of the partnership and consider your own identity throughout that time.

3. After finishing those two lists, it's time to consider what lies next. List the aspects of your most recent relationship that you would like to

keep and those you would want to let go of. Don't use more than one page for everyone.

4. Lastly, think about what you might do differently in a future partnership. At the top of every page, write "What exactly I Will Do Differently subsequent Time". Put down any steps you want to take to increase your chances of establishing a lasting connection on that page. This may include seeing a therapist or reading self-help literature.

After completing this procedure, you will recognize the significance of this connection in your life's path. It is anticipated that you will have gained further insight into your identity, your preferences for a partner, and how to improve your romantic life moving forward.

Chapter Four

Handling Persistent Problems

Sometimes you get a curveball in life. Most of the time, you can catch it and go on. Other times, it is more difficult to get beyond a stressful situation. Taking care of an aging parent, experiencing financial insecurity, or parenting a kid with special needs or chronic health conditions are examples of these kinds of obstacles. They could also include handling a supervisor that makes you want to give up your job. Stress from any of these difficulties may arise and has to be properly controlled.

Taking Care of Parents

Our parents grow older together with us. With any luck, they will be able to enjoy their post-retirement years while being fit, active, and self-sufficient. Others find that life wears us down, and our parents need a little help to get by each day.

This may be as easy as hiring a maid to cook and do errands, or it could be more significant like hiring a full-time caregiver—who could be you—to provide round-the-clock support. For any parent, the role reversal might provide difficulties. Realizing that your kid should take care of you rather than the other way around must be a depressing realization. Furthermore, children may believe that their efforts are insufficient due to the sense of duty and obligation they have toward their parents.

Exercises Focused on Bodily Motion

The movement practice that follows is intended to assist you in managing your anxiety when you see your parent aging and need assistance or care. You might feel accomplished after a successful exercise and feel fantastic afterward. You already have an outlet if you follow an exercise regimen. To maximize the benefits of the workout, you might include this in your usual regimen.

1. All you need for this activity are comfortable shoes and clothing, as well as appropriate gear that will enable you to confront all weather conditions.

2. Go for a stroll outdoors, come rain or shine. This stroll is more intended to improve mental clarity and mood than it is to target fitness.

3. Walk for at least fifteen minutes, at a fast pace.

4. This duration of time will work on certain days. In other cases, you may need to walk for an hour to reach a state of satisfaction.

Experiencing Uncertainty About Money

It's enough to keep you up at night and brooding all day when you don't have enough money to pay your expenses and sustain your lifestyle. It's difficult not to think about money when you're fixated on finding ways to get more of it.

Practice Journaling

The goal of this writing exercise is to solve problems and create a strategy that will provide you with some guidance and hope for your long-term financial stability.

1. Write out your short-term (the next three months) financial goals and aspirations.
2. Carry out the identical action for a duration of one to five years. Among the topics to think about are:

- *Do you want to purchase a home?*

- *Do you want to relocate to a different neighborhood?*

- *Would you want to go on a fantastic vacation?*

- *Do you want to establish a personal retirement fund?*

3. Write down how you plan to accomplish your objectives when you've documented them. Among the options are:

- *A wage increase or a new position with more money.*

- *A side job to pay off debt or build an emergency reserve shrinking your house to save money and improve your financial security*

4. Next, choose one of your financial goals from Step 1 and relate it to at least one of your Step 3 money management techniques.

5. The last stage is to create a brief list of five specific objectives that will enable you to use one of those management techniques. Set a deadline for each action that will help you stay on pace to meet at least one of your financial objectives.

- For instance, you should provide at least three justifications for your merit if you want to seek a raise. What improvements have you made to your business? When did you surpass everyone's expectations? Alternatively, it's possible that you've done your homework and discovered that your pay is less than the industry median.

- Make a small list of possible side gigs, such as dog walking, home sitting, helping with errands, retail, customer service, etc., if you plan to get a side gig. Next, make profiles on the appropriate job-seeking websites, including Indeed, and Wag! TaskRabbit, etc., and begin your search.

Unhappy Marriage

If your marriage or relationship is miserable, you probably wonder how much longer you should put up with it before ending it. Perhaps you've decided to remain and are unsure of how to make things better. It's simple for the positive aspects of your life to be eclipsed in an unhappy marriage by the difficulties of cohabiting with someone who doesn't make you happy.

Practice Journaling

Don't let your marriage determine your level of happiness until you decide it. Joy is a state of being. You can be joyful even if your life isn't "good." There are benefits to consciously choosing to be appreciative. People who express thankfulness are less stressed, according to research. Being thankful also enables you to put your attention on the good things in life, which might help you ignore the "bad" things.

1. Fill out each of the following index card prompts, one for each phrase. For every prompt, you may provide many responses:

- Upon reflection about my family, I am appreciative of:
- Upon reflection on my work, I am appreciative of:
- I am appreciative of the chance to produce:
- Regarding my house, I am appreciative of:
- Regarding my well-being, I am appreciative of
- Upon reflection on my finances, I am appreciative of :
- In general, I am appreciative of:

2. After finishing these cards, place them in a bag you carry every day and secure them with a staple, clip, or rubber band.

3. Refer to your list whenever you're feeling down to help you change your outlook and cheer yourself up.

Loneliness

Loneliness is increasing even with all the virtual relationships that social media offers. Humans still want in-person engagement, even in this day and age when social media platforms like Facebook, Instagram, and WhatsApp groups allow you to stay current on the activities of your loved ones, favorite celebrities, and relatives. Furthermore, a lot of us—including myself—spend our workdays alone at home in our jammies since so many people work remotely.

Exercises Focused on Bodily Motion

Let's concentrate on movement to assist you keep a human connection. Locate at least one group of individuals who share your enjoyment of a certain physical activity. A Meetup group of walkers, a salsa class at your neighborhood YMCA, a cycling club sponsored by a local bike shop, or a trek with your local Sierra Club are just a few options for your group exercise.

1. List three enjoyable physical activities that you engage in.

2. Check online to see whether companies provide the sorts of activities you have listed. If yoga is on your list, for instance, it ought to be simple to locate a class close by.

3. If you're not into courses, check out what local clubs are currently active in your region using the Internet Meetup platform.

There are organizations for hiking and tennis, for instance, or maybe Ultimate Frisbee is more your style.

4. Whatever you decide to do, it's a fantastic way to meet individuals who share your interests and lays the groundwork for conversation.

5. The companionship you encounter will help you feel less alone even if you don't make pals. Not to mention the perk of feeling good about doing something you adore.

6. If none of that is sufficient, you can also experience a sense of fulfillment and success from your increased cardiovascular and physical fitness.

Taking Care of a Kid with Special Needs

It's challenging to raise kids. Special needs children are particularly challenging to raise. The level of care your kid needs will determine how stressed you are. Another influence is the level of support you get from your social circle, family, and local resources. Whatever your circumstances, it's simple to store tension in your shoulders and neck, which may result in headaches, persistent discomfort, stiffness, soreness, and a restricted range of motion.

Exercises Focused on Bodily Motion

The goal of this movement exercise is to assist you in releasing some of the tension in your upper back, shoulders, and neck. Although you may do this exercise while seated, I advise you to stand instead of sit as most people spend far too much time in chairs already. Additionally, standing might improve blood circulation.

1. Take a relaxed stance, hang your arms freely by your sides, and face forward with your open

palms. (If seated, put your hands on your thighs in an upward position.)

2. Raise your shoulders in line with your ears.

3. Roll your shoulders in a circle, starting from the rear and moving forward, down, and finally back up near your ears.

4. Repeat step 3 five times at a slow pace.

5. Next, roll your shoulders in the other way using a similar motion. Start by rolling forward, then roll down toward your back, and finally roll back up to your shoulders.

6. Repeat step 5 five times at a slow pace.

7. 7. Let your shoulders drop.

8. Lastly, take a deep breath through your nose and raise your shoulders toward your ears gradually. Then, take a leisurely breath out and lower your shoulders back down at the same rate.

9. Five times, repeat step 8.

Living With a Spouse Who Struggles with Mental Health Problems

It is really difficult to see someone we love battle mental health problems. It may be emotionally and psychologically taxing to have a close, personal connection with someone who is mentally ill. It is difficult to connect with them because of their erratic and unexpected emotions and actions, which may be a symptom of their mental health problem. Living with someone who has a mental health problem may be challenging since their actions and feelings don't always accurately represent who they are or how they are feeling. Rather, the mental health conditions people battle have an impact on their emotions and behaviors.

Practice Meditation

It takes a great deal of patience to be the object of emotional upheaval. It takes a change in viewpoint that isolates the person behind the sickness from their behavior to actively love them. Keeping your attention on their positive traits is essential. It is even more crucial to tell them. The main goal of this exercise is to pay attention to the good. Remind yourself of the enjoyable moments you have recently had when your spouse exhibits signs that might cause you to get irritated, angry, or wounded. Although I can't guarantee it would ease your situation, it could help you concentrate on your relationship during difficult times when it's difficult to remember your shared love.

1. Recall some enjoyable moments you two had. The more recent the occasion, the better, as it will help you realize that happy moments may

still happen in the future as well as the present. Selecting a point in the far past might cause you to focus more on what you have lost than what you now have.

2. Express this moment to your significant other to redirect their attention to the enjoyable experiences you have had. If they're not ready to hear it right now, concentrate more on your thoughts and less on theirs.

It's possible that your spouse needs to hear about these good qualities of your relationship and their personality to concentrate on getting healthy. In addition, it may give them hope for the future and make them feel loved when they might not have felt deserving of it.

Managing a Chronic Disease

It may be very stressful to have a chronic condition, such as multiple sclerosis, diabetes, or cancer. It has the power to change the emphasis from enjoying the little moments in life to striving to be the best version of yourself. Medical procedures or prescribed medicines may be necessary to manage your sickness. Maybe you're just enduring your disease.

Regardless of your physical limits, having a positive connection with your body is facilitated by feeling "able." Physical stamina and strength are increased by movement. Additionally, depending on the kind of condition you may have, it can lessen the frequency and intensity of symptoms. Finally, the pleasure neurotransmitters dopamine and serotonin may be released by movement.

Exercises Focused on Bodily Motion

This movement practice is centered on moving for a minimum of ten minutes. (Be careful to pick an exercise program that is appropriate for you by speaking with your healthcare physician.) This is an activity that you may do at any time of the day.

- Walking is a fantastic option as it can be done anytime, anyplace, and with little equipment or ability. If you have physical restrictions that make walking difficult, talk to your healthcare physician about the best solutions for you.

- Swimming is yet another fantastic choice. Strengthening oneself by moving in the water is often simpler and more efficient than doing it on land. Water has a built-in resistance and buoyancy that lessen the force on joints. If you are physically capable and do not know how to swim, picking up this life-saving skill can help you concentrate on your body's power and capabilities rather than its limits. If swimming isn't a possibility, consider enrolling in a water-based movement class. Before committing, make sure to request a free trial class in case you find it difficult to complete or incorporate into your daily schedule.

Unavoidable Stress

Chapter Five

Dealing with Situations That Affect Your Life

Significant life experiences are those that alter our identities and self-perceptions. When a loved one passes away, we lose our jobs, or we have to relocate due to a natural catastrophe, these are the times when we feel the strongest emotions. These big life events take us off guard and profoundly alter our lives.

A child's Delivery or Adoption

Greetings to the newest member of your family! The day has finally arrived after much anticipation and preparation, and you are ecstatic. But even amid your happiness, it's natural to feel overwhelmed while you get used to having this new person in your life. There are many factors to take into account when you're forging a relationship with your child—someone you will adore without condition and forever—including the shift in your daily routine and the added costs. It's important to find a good coping mechanism for the stress of being a new parent.

Practice Journaling

Writing in your journal about your emotions, ideas, and experiences with your kid helps you as a parent to process the experience and gives you a safe space to release your worries. Before you start, consider if this is something that you want to keep to yourself or whether you want to share it with your kid in the future. Your choice may influence the topics you write about. Whatever you choose, I strongly advise you to organize your posts so that you may address whatever is on your mind every day.

You are free to use whatever structure you choose, but if you are stuck and don't know where to begin, I've included a guideline for your contributions below.

- What happened place today? Just jot down any remarkable events that happened in whatever format you like.
- What action do I take in response? This part focuses on your response to whatever occurred today since you want to pay attention to what you did.
- My thoughts about it. Naming your feelings may help you get your emotions out before bed and better understand who you are as a parent. Parenting is an emotional job. You'll be able to sleep better and clear your head by doing this.
- What I discovered today about my kid or myself as a parent. Finding the lesson in the ordinary

gives your life significance, from the spectacular parenting moments to the routine ones. It changes the way you see these moments.

- What would I change or keep the same? Well, if you don't alter your behavior, there's no need to pick up a lesson. Putting the daily lessons into practice, no matter how little, will not only help you become a better parent but also provide a chance for personal development.

Bereavement

Everybody experiences grief at some point in their lives, and losing a parent is no exception. The death of a parent is often a turning moment in your relationship, regardless of its form. It's one of those times when your life's narrative has a before and after. Grief may be overwhelming and never-ending for some individuals. Others discover that the greatest way to commemorate their parent is to go ahead and make the most of every day. It simply depends on the individual who is grieving. Either manner is ok.

Practice Journaling

It's important to understand that there are no right or incorrect ways to deal with a parent's passing. Nonetheless, a well-respected model that depicts the phases of mourning exists. According to Elisabeth Kübler-Ross' paradigm, human experiences are arranged as follows: denial, anger, bargaining, depression, and acceptance. Let's review these steps to help you structure your ideas and process your emotions before we go into the writing exercise.

Denial: This is the outcome of the first shock you experience upon your parent's death, even if you were prepared for their illness or advanced age. It seldom comes readily when it does. You have to speak with them nevertheless.

Fury: We try to make sense of this new reality by blaming someone or something, or by becoming angry with the world in general.

Haggling: A feeling of motivation to alter how you navigate life's path. You can feel guilty about saying or doing things differently before your parent passed away and vow that you will make amends in the future.

Depression: An inability to eat, excessive napping, and a lack of drive or energy are all signs of depression. To go to the subsequent stage of mourning, it is essential to manage these symptoms.

Acceptance: The last stage is more about accepting that this person is no longer with us and that life will not be the same in the future than it is about accepting what occurred.

To write every day for the first thirty days, start by writing at least once per day. You may process what you are going through and find language for your feelings and thoughts about your loved one by writing your way through your loss. You may decide to write less often as you process the loss and go through the mourning process.

Even though you may not feel like writing every day, keeping a diary is a great method to process your loss and offers you a place to store your emotions so you can go about your day or go to sleep at night.

It's ok to write a single word, like "angry," or a brief statement, like "All I want to do is cry." Putting your emotions on paper can help you release them from your heart and mind. Maintaining a journal can help you deal with your experiences, but it won't make mourning any easier.

Demise From Work

We want to feel in control when it comes to our jobs. Your self-perception might be significantly impacted by being fired or remarried. A lot of individuals associate their identity with their work, along with their sense of competence and self-worth. A job loss puts such emotions in jeopardy. It's critical to keep in mind that you are qualified for both one job and another throughout this period.

Practice Meditation

Change your perspective of this event from one of a loss to one of an opportunity. Regaining confidence for the next job hunt depends on completing this first step. The goal of this exercise is to recognize your negative self-talk and transform it into something good. It will be time for your reframing if you find yourself believing that you will not be hired.

1. Consider what and why you would want to work at your future employment. Maybe you've always wanted to try something else, and now is the ideal moment to reconsider your professional path.

2. Consider your ideal employer or employers, and prepare an application that will help you get a job, even if it's not the one you've had before.

3. Does the new vocation or employment call for any more schooling or training?

4. What changes should you make to your resume to make it stand out so you can get that dream job?

4. What takeaways from your prior company and work experience, and how can you use those takeaways in your future role?

Remind yourself of your strengths and qualities as an employee to be confident and upbeat. Refer back to these ideas whenever you find yourself questioning your skills or potential.

A Disastrous Natural Event

Mother Nature and life are so unpredictable. You could know others who haven't been as fortunate as you if you've survived a natural catastrophe like an earthquake or storm. Whatever your fate, experiencing a natural catastrophe might leave you with PTSD, despair, or anxiety, depending on what happened to you. Developing coping mechanisms while tidying up or attempting to resume your routine is a sensible strategy.

Exercises Focused on Bodily Motion

The goal of this practice is to help you establish a peaceful connection with nature. You must breathe steadily and evenly while doing the next stance, known as an asana in yoga terminology, and you should not experience any discomfort to ensure your safety.

If you consider yourself a bit of a yogi, then spend fifteen minutes doing a sequence of positions outdoors. Bring a yoga mat if necessary, and dress according to the weather. If it's too chilly outside, do this in front of an open window to maintain a connection to the outside world.

If this is your first experience with yoga, you will begin with a simple standing posture that will help you get familiar with the grounding, centering, and soothing effects of the practice.

You will learn the Mountain stance (Tadasana), an excellent "resting" stance that serves as the base for all standing poses. It promotes calmness and helps with posture and balance.

1. Put on relaxed attire. It's better to go barefoot if the weather allows.

2. Place your heels slightly apart and your big toes together. Step with your feet hip-width apart, parallel, and your toes pointing forward if you feel unbalanced by this.

3. Spread your toes widely apart and firmly plant all four-foot corners in the earth. 4. Press your shoulder blades toward your back and pull your lower ribs forward, keeping them away from your ears.

4. With your palms pointing forward, dangle your arms freely by your sides. Keep your face relaxed and your chin in line with the floor. 6.

Assume a tall, straight stance and position your body such that a string passes between your spine and the top of your head from the middle of your pelvis.

7. Breathe in via the nose and out of the mouth as you take five calm, deep breaths while counting to three. Repeat.

Severe Sickness

We often take our health for granted, even though it is very valuable—that is until we get sick and need medical attention. We are forced to confront our mortality by anything like a heart attack, cancer diagnosis, or other life-threatening disease. After you've recovered, you could also have to adjust to a new world. Changes to your new daily routine could be necessary for your long-term health as well as while you recover. Thinking positively may increase your chances of recovering, according to research, and it can also make you feel more hopeful about the future.

Practice Meditation

A meditation exercise is beneficial to combat the worry, anxiety, grief, and emotions of loss that may accompany a severe disease because it alters our self-perception. I advise you to complete steps 1 and 2 before starting any kind of medicine or medical therapy for your condition.

1. Start by seeing yourself as a warrior overcoming your sickness.
2. Shut your eyes, see every cell in your body as a fighter, your sickness as a punching bag, and visualize your cells striking this sickness.
3. Once you've had that mental vision, start your therapy or take your prescription.

4. Hold this boxing picture in your mind for the duration of your therapy if it entails doing more than just swallowing a medication.

The following exercise should be performed as soon as you wake up each morning.

1. Visualize a future in which you are well from your disease and consider the first action you will take upon recovering.
2. Pay attention to that day, that activity, and your anticipated feelings, regardless of the nature of the activity.
3. Experience that happiness. Experience your independence. And trust that it is possible.

Toddler Demise

Because it defies the laws of nature, losing a child is especially painful. I must admit that there is nothing in this book that can make up for the agony of this kind of loss, but it can help ease some of the stress that comes with handling all the responsibilities associated with a loved one's passing.

Practice Journaling

Although grieving is a process that may not ever fully finish, this writing exercise will allow you to honor your child's life and provide a release for your emotions. You are going to keep a grieving notebook, which you should use anytime you feel compelled to write.

1. The objective is to write every day about your thoughts and recollections; there won't be a time or page restriction for the first thirty days.

2. You may write as much or as little as you choose, but you should think about writing every day as it will help you process your profoundly

felt emotions by allowing you to connect with and express them.

You may start to add more structure to your writing after the first month. That being said, grieving is a personal experience, and you should feel free to make your notebook as unstructured as you need it to be. When you're prepared for more direction on what and when to write, take into account the following:

1. Keep writing every day throughout this time, but choose one memory of your kid each day and concentrate on one emotion associated with it.

2. You have up to 30 minutes to write, but you may write for as long as you want.

3. You are free to write at whatever time of day that works best for you.

4. permit yourself to mourn every day, even if your family and friends have returned to their routine and life has resumed as usual.

5. Even if life is going on, your sadness won't go away quickly. You may be able to get through the remainder of your day if you honor your sentiments.

6. Keep going through this procedure for as long as you think it's required.

Chapter Six

Living Alongside Past or Current Trauma

Every individual reacts to adversity differently. While most individuals go on with their lives, others find it difficult to do so. Trauma may be harmful to one's body, mind, emotions, or spirituality. Shock and denial are examples of short-term reactions. Trauma may eventually lead to interpersonal issues, mental anguish, and flashbacks. Physical symptoms are prevalent and include headaches, nausea, changes in appetite, and sleeplessness.

Post-traumatic stress disorder (PTSD) is an anxiety condition that affects stress hormones and the physical, emotional, and psychological responses of the body to stress. It is another reaction to trauma. Years after a terrible occurrence, post-traumatic stress disorder (PTSD) may produce severe responses to the memories of the incident.

Childhood Sexual Abuse or Assault

In a perfect world, the people in children's lives would always adore and take care of them. But the mistreatment of children does occur sometimes. The worst form of breach of trust is when the individuals who are supposed to be protecting you subject them to emotional, psychological, or physical abuse. Lifelong psychological and emotional repercussions may arise from this.

Practice Meditation

It's critical to reconsider how you interpret these occurrences within the broader framework of your life. Changing your way of thinking to make this your go-to answer could take some time. It's also important to keep in mind that you cannot go back in time, and pondering about hypothetical scenarios makes it difficult to get beyond the past. The future and your perception of the things that have occurred to you in the past are things that you can alter. The goal of this exercise is to change the way you think about your part in what occurred to you.

1. To begin with, bear in mind that you were not responsible for your safety when you were a youngster. Adults and others in your immediate vicinity must look out for and protect you.
2. This was someone abusing their influence or position to take advantage of someone weaker than they were. It's entirely unrelated to you.
3. You were not worthy of being harmed as a kid, regardless of what you did or who you were.
4. To help you remember this, remind yourself, "It wasn't my fault," each time you recall what

happened to you. This was not anything I deserved.

5. Reminding yourself that "I cannot change what happened to me then, but I can choose how I respond now" is equally crucial. This can help offset the lack of control you had as a youngster and offer you a greater sense of control both now and in the future.

Childhood Bullying

Bullying is defined as aggressive, unwelcome behavior—verbal, social, or physical—that hurts or controls another person by taking advantage of a power imbalance. Long-term repetition of the conduct might include name-calling, physical or verbal abuse, humiliation, rumors, threats, and purposeful exclusion from a group. Being bullied as a youngster may be very stressful and have long-lasting effects.

Practice Journaling

You may process what occurred and get beyond a terrible incident by writing about it. It's possible that you wrote about being bullied as a youngster, but it must have been quite upsetting to feel powerless at the time. Looking back as an adult bestows upon you the wisdom of perspective. With the aid of this exercise, you will be able to process your ongoing thoughts over the bullying you endured and regain the authority that was taken away from you.

1. Write about the first bullying episode you can recall.

2. You will respond to the following questions as you write the account of what transpired:

   - *Who mistreated you?*

   - *Where and when did it take place?*

   - *Who was there when the event happened?*

- *You reported it to whom?*

- *How did they act?*

- *You should document your reasoning if you choose not to report it to anybody.*

3. You will write about your sentiments at the time after you have described the events of one occurrence.

  - *Did you feel angry?*

  - *Did you experience frustration?*

  - *Did you shed a tear?*

  - *Did you do anything at the time to help you feel better?*

4. Write down what you would have liked to say or done to the person or persons who were harassing you at the time.

5. Write your thoughts regarding the occurrence right now.

- *Do the same emotions still affect you?*

- *Have you learned any lessons from the experience that you are* applying to your current situation?

6. After that, you will respond to the following query:

- *If you saw the person who bullied you today, what would you say* to them?

7. Compose a letter to them explaining your thoughts.

8. Write the following statement after the letter: "What you did to me will no longer control my present or my future."

9. Read this letter into a mirror when you've finished writing it, just as you would if you were reading it to the person you wrote it to.

10. Now grab all the written pages and tear them apart. Taking them to pieces is a metaphor for letting go of this memory and its effect on you.

11. Place the torn paper into your wood-burning fireplace and watch it burn if you have one. If not, dispose of it in the recycling or trash container.

Once this process is over, you should feel relieved and maybe even like you've come to a point where you can let go of a difficult memory.

Vehicle Accident

Being in a vehicle accident may be distressing regardless of who is at blame or if anybody was hurt. Whether or whether you are the one driving, the incident may make you anxious about getting into a vehicle again.

Mindfulness-Based Practices

Try the following mindfulness practice to help you overcome the anxiety you may have whenever you think about the accident or even consider getting back into a car or other motorized vehicle.

You have probably driven a lot of automobiles in your lifetime, and you probably have pleasant recollections of road trips or specific vehicles. You will concentrate on those pleasant recollections for this activity. Setting the memories of this one horrific event in its right perspective is the aim.

1. Look for a peaceful, cozy spot to sit.
2. Set a timer to notify you after ten minutes.
3. Shut your eyes and recall your most treasured road trip experience.
4. Commence by recalling the thrill of preparation for the journey.
5. Next, concentrate on the actual journey.

- *How far did you go?*
- *With whom did you travel?*
- *Which stops did you make a new route?*

- *Which vacation experience did you like the most?*

6. Before the allotted ten minutes expire, try to spend as much time as possible thinking back on your fondest memory.

7. When you're feeling nervous about a vehicle accident in the future, go back to this enjoyable road trip experience.

8. When the emotions start to surface, shut your eyes, count to five while inhaling and exhaling deeply, and then open your eyes. Recall your best road trip memory.

Your anxious sensations will ultimately give way to feelings of serenity and enjoyment as you practice mindfulness, and the trauma of the automobile crash should finally disappear.

Adult-onset Abuse or Assault

Our sense of safety and control might be permanently impacted by any personal violation we encounter in life. A single event may have a lasting effect on your mental state; repeated abuse can be far more detrimental to your emotional and mental health than it is to any physical harm you may have sustained. You could feel vulnerable, helpless, and furious at the same time.

Exercises Focused on Bodily Motion

This practice is meant to help you regain your feeling of control and power, as well as to help you feel stronger and maybe safer. There will be two parts to this practice. Push-ups will be the first exercise to strengthen the upper body. To improve your coordination and confidence, the second section will consist of a boxing practice.

The goal of the combination exercise will be to restore your confidence and make you feel stronger.

1. Start by dressing comfortably so that you can move about easily.

2. Take a correct push-up stance.

3. Continue by doing one to ten push-ups in a set.

4. You will do as many as you can for the first three days, and then you will add one more every three days until you reach ten.

5. Adding another set of push-ups to your program will be the aim if you already do them as part of your exercise regimen.

6. Do not go above three sets, regardless of the quantity you choose.

7. Carry out these everyday workouts for a month.

Once you have completed your push-ups, go to the second portion of this workout. A lot of individuals discover that boxing offers them a sense of confidence and strength. It could also aid in your boxing skill development! Find a nearby gym that provides boxing instruction, if at all feasible, and sign up for a one-month course. For that month, show up to class two or three times a week. If taking a boxing class is out of your price range or time constraints, you may practice shadowboxing at home by practicing striking the person who assaulted you in the mirror:

1. Turn to face the mirror to start.
2. Take a tall stance, place your feet shoulder-width apart, and keep your arms at your sides in a comfortable manner.
3. Use both hands to make fists.
4. Begin striking the air with your dominant hand (use your left hand if you're left-handed, and your right hand if you're right-handed).

5. Use your other hand in the same manner. You'll use each hand to deliver ten punches in turn.

6. You may add more sets of this exercise as your strength and ability increase.

7. For a month, repeat this exercise two to three times a week.

It should be mentioned that no guarantee having strength would have prevented what occurred to you from happening. Helping you feel stronger in the present is the focus here, not the past.

Infidelity

A fundamental requirement of marital vows and a fundamental expectation of both parties is faithfulness. When someone violates that commitment, it might alter your perspective of the relationship and jeopardize your dreams for the two of you. We often question our actions and inactions when there is a breach of trust. You could also be wondering how it was that you were unaware of this.

Practice Meditation

Feeling inadequate for your relationship might arise from infidelity. The first step in this reflective practice is to concentrate on not placing the blame for what transpired on yourself.

1. Regardless of how challenging your relationship has been, your spouse decided to be unfaithful; there were many other options.

2. You do not have to bear the blame for your partner's infidelity if you accept responsibility for improving the relationship's future.

3. Tell yourself three times, "The air was not my fault," if you sense that you are at fault.

Reminding yourself that you are enough is the second element of this technique.

1. Remind yourself that nothing about you is to blame for this conduct if you catch yourself believing that it wouldn't have occurred if you were more fun, had a nicer face, or had a better shape.

2. Say to yourself three times, "I am enough," to remind yourself of your value whenever you feel that anything is lacking that led to your spouse cheating. I deserve to know the truth. I am deserving of loyalty.

Faced Family Illness During Formative Years

If a parent or sibling suffered from a terrible disease while you were a youngster, you could feel that you did not have the same childhood experiences as other kids. It's possible that you had more responsibilities than other children when you were younger, or that your parent was unable to fulfill some of your wishes. You can even think that childhood was stolen from you.

Practice Journaling

The goal of this writing exercise is to assist you in processing the feelings and ideas you have about your early experiences growing up in a home where there was a significant illness in one or more members of your immediate family.

1. If you did not always experience sickness as a kid, start this activity by writing a page describing your early years before the disease became a regular part of your life.

- *What activities did your family members like doing before they became sick?*

- *Write about a treasured memory you have of them before their sickness.*

2. Compose a page describing your first thoughts upon learning that your parent or sibling was unwell.

  - *How did you find out?*
  - *By whom was it told?*
  - *When you were informed, where were you?*

3. You will discuss what changed once sickness entered your family's life on the next page.

- *How has your sibling or parent changed?*

- *How has your bond with your parent or sibling evolved?*

- *Were you required to pay them hospital visits? What changes have you seen in your family's role?*

- *Did you have to assume more responsibilities at home?*

- *Did the illness of your parent or sibling make you feel sad or angry?*
- *Did you think that life was unjust?*

4. You will discuss any life lessons you took away from your experience on the last page. In what ways has the experience shaped who you are? This part will assist you in changing your perspective from what you lost as a youngster to what you have gained as an adult.

- *In what ways did the experience help you become a better kid or sibling?*
- *In what ways has the experience strengthened or deepened your gratitude?*
- *In what ways has this experience benefited you in your current life?*

Combative Wars

Trauma is inherent in war by definition. Combat in the military requires troops to function under extreme stress. Regardless of one's level of training, facing the possibility of dying or causing the death of others may have a lasting psychological impact.

Practice Meditation

The goal of this activity is to lessen the stress brought on by battle experience rather than to cure PTSD. By practicing mindfulness, you may create a mental barrier between yourself and your fight memories, increasing your sense of control over them. You may cultivate mindfulness by directing your attention to the meaningful connections in your life as well as the things that make you happy right now.

Practice mindfulness and direct your attention to the present moment with this exercise. By concentrating on the present, you will address the past. You can perform this workout anywhere, and you need to strive to include it in your daily regimen.

1. Allocate five minutes to do this workout thrice a day. Allocate time for the start, middle, and finish of the day. This technique may also be used at any other time of day when you need to concentrate yourself.

2. Shut your eyes to start. Take a long, leisurely, deep breath in, and pay attention to your breathing. As your diaphragm expands, feel the air enter your lungs via your nose. Then, as the air exits your body, notice how it begins to relax.

3. Take a moment to concentrate on the smells you are now inhaling.

    - *Does food or drink smell to you?*
    - *Is there someone's perfume on, or is the place scented?*

4. Keep your eyes closed and concentrate on what you are hearing for a minute, all the while taking calm, deep breaths. Take in all of the noises around you.

- *Whose voices are those?*
- *What background sounds are there?*

5. Open your eyes gradually and take a minute to scan your surroundings.

- *Have you seen something or somebody that you were previously unaware of?*

6. Take one last, deep breath to bring the session to a close and resume your day.

Chapter Seven

An Appropriate Reaction to Stress

One of the first researchers on stress, Hans Selye, famously said, "It's not stress that kills us, it's our stress reaction." There is no inherent good or bad in stress. However, there is a clear correlation between your ability to manage stress and the different psychological, emotional, and physical effects you encounter.

Controlling your reaction to stressful events is the aim since eliminating stress from your life is neither feasible nor reasonable. Numerous functioning systems in your body respond, including the digestive, respiratory, neurological, endocrine, cardiovascular, and reproductive systems. All people have a set of stress reactions, however.

You may maintain composure and concentrate in the face of everyday pressures by learning to recognize the things that set off your stress responses and become conscious of your reactions. Enhancing your emotional toughness might also aid in your recovery from being knocked off balance by a big, unanticipated incident.

Acute stress is the term for the nervousness you have before making a speech. It makes you more aware of your surroundings, and if you can use that awareness to your advantage, it may improve your performance. Stress may become counterproductive if you don't handle it properly. You can have nausea, dizziness, sweaty palms, or stomach aches in addition to not doing as well as you had intended. As soon as the acute tension subsides, your body will become peaceful again.

Chronic continuous stress is not a healthy way to live. Your body was not designed to remain in a constant state of hyperarousal. Prolonged exposure to stress chemicals such as cortisol and adrenaline might raise your risk of cardiovascular disease, diabetes, obesity, and hypertension. You can feel overwhelmed by ongoing stress and become agitated, easily agitated, or more likely to weep. Headaches, gastrointestinal issues, and tense muscles in your jaw, neck, or shoulders are some other symptoms.

Long-term stress exposure may have psychological effects such as anxiety and depression. Regardless of the origin of your stress, whether it is your job, relationships, finances, or a catastrophic event, this book aims to help you develop a healthy stress response. The severity and length of an event influence how destructive stress is, but you may adapt to difficult and demanding circumstances by learning how to reframe what you're going through. By using comprehensive stress management techniques, you may start to regulate your body's and mind's reactions.

Techniques for Stress Management

There are many constructive strategies to handle stress. The stress management and prevention situations covered in this book's many parts are not all-inclusive. The intention behind this book is to maybe help you find someone going through something similar, no matter what you're going through. Even if there is a prescribed exercise for every situation, you can discover that you like one kind of answer more than another. You could find that moving helps you cope with stress more effectively than anything else, or maybe writing is the greatest method for you to process your feelings.

Just keep in mind that there isn't a single right method to handle a difficult circumstance.

Considering each reader's individual stress threshold and favorite pastimes, I hope they can all find something that works. A regular stress-reduction regimen may benefit from including some of the activities I've listed, such as writing about feelings, mindfulness techniques, and physical activity like yoga. Regular use of stress-reduction techniques lowers susceptibility to stress and increases emotional resilience.

Moving Ahead

Every day we deal with stressful events such as a challenging test, getting stopped in traffic, or issues in our relationships with the people we care about. Due to the unpredictable nature of life, we will all eventually encounter a difficult situation that knocks us off balance and leaves us feeling overwhelmed, such as a loss in the family or an illness. Building emotional resilience is crucial for this reason. We can emotionally be ready for life's obstacles before they arise, therefore waiting for unpleasant things to happen is not enough to cope with them.

It's critical to identify stress-reduction techniques and apply them to your daily activities. Being aware at the beginning of the day is a terrific way to feel peaceful, focused, and balanced. Because of the detrimental effects of our increasingly sedentary lifestyle, medical professionals claim that "sitting is the new smoking." In light of this, getting moving is a fantastic way to start the day. It might cause your blood to flow and wake you up. Sitting in front of a gadget is also bad for our mental health and cognitive performance.

Getting some exercise throughout the workday is an excellent remedy. Another great method for reducing stress is to journal, particularly if you write about thankfulness. Putting ideas and emotions on paper helps you bring them to mind, and writing facilitates this process. To let go of your day's tension, unwind, and get a good night's sleep, you may include stress management practices into your nighttime routine.

A healthy stress reaction is possible. You may anticipate and prepare for your stress reaction by being aware of the things that set it off. Even if you don't anticipate it, you can accomplish anything and overcome any obstacle in life when you learn stress-reduction techniques that keep you content and in good physical and mental health.

Conclusion

The findings from the Stress in America study underscore a concerning trend: millennials and Gen Xers experience higher levels of stress compared to baby boomers, and women tend to report higher stress levels than men. Moreover, stress associated with systemic issues such as racism, homophobia, or sexism likely exacerbates the overall stress burden, particularly for marginalized individuals.

Addressing stress in our lives is paramount, given its pervasive impact on mental and physical well-being. While complete eradication of stress may be unattainable, there are proactive steps we can take to manage and alleviate its effects. This may involve cultivating resilience through practices such as mindfulness, meditation, or therapy. Additionally, fostering supportive relationships, prioritizing self-care, and establishing healthy boundaries can contribute to a more balanced and resilient approach to stress management.

Furthermore, societal interventions aimed at addressing systemic inequalities and promoting inclusivity can help mitigate stressors related to discrimination and marginalization. By advocating for social justice, promoting diversity and inclusion, and actively challenging oppressive systems, we can work towards creating a more equitable and less stressful society for all individuals.

In essence, while stress may be an unavoidable aspect of life, it is within our power to equip ourselves with the tools and support systems necessary to navigate its challenges effectively. Through a combination of individual resilience-building strategies and collective efforts to address systemic stressors, we can strive toward a healthier and more resilient society overall.